T0090650

The *Rapture* DECEPTION

Deacon Floyd Fleshman

WESTBOW
PRESS®
A DIVISION OF THOMAS NELSON
& ZONDERVAN

Copyright © 2016 Deacon Floyd Fleshman.

All rights reserved. No part of this book may be used
or reproduced by any means, graphic, electronic, or
mechanical, including photocopying, recording, taping or
by any information storage retrieval system without the
written permission of the author except in the case of brief
quotations embodied in critical articles and reviews.

All scriptures are taken from the _Scofield Reference Bible_,
the authorized King James Version. Copyright 1909, 1917.
Copyright renewed 1937, 1945, by Oxford University Press, Inc.

WestBow Press books may be ordered through
booksellers or by contacting:

WestBow Press
A Division of Thomas Nelson & Zondervan
1663 Liberty Drive
Bloomington, IN 47403
www.westbowpress.com
1 (866) 928-1240

Because of the dynamic nature of the Internet, any web
addresses or links contained in this book may have changed
since publication and may no longer be valid. The views
expressed in this work are solely those of the author and do
not necessarily reflect the views of the publisher, and the
publisher hereby disclaims any responsibility for them.

Any people depicted in stock imagery provided
by Thinkstock are models, and such images are
being used for illustrative purposes only.
Certain stock imagery © Thinkstock.

ISBN: 978-1-5127-2756-2 (sc)
ISBN: 978-1-5127-2757-9 (e)

Print information available on the last page.

WestBow Press rev. date: 2/11/2016

Contents

Method of Writing

The method of writing I am using is to use the word of God in an order that can easily be understood by the Lord's people when the rapture shall occur. II Timothy 2:15 tells us to rightly divide the word of truth. When the word of God is being divided wrongly, it should be corrected by the word of God (II Timothy 3:16).

When reading this book, you will need your Bible to use as a reference. May God bless all of you who believe His word.

Deacon Floyd W. Fleshman

Introduction

This book has been written so that the truth is known about the second coming of our Lord to gather together His church. Man calls this event the rapture. Christians have been deceived into thinking that it can happen at anytime. This book has been composed to show, without a doubt, when that time shall occur.

My Favorite Scripture

Romans 3:4, "God forbid: yea, Let God be true, but every man a liar; as it is written, That thou mightest be justified in thy sayings, and mightest overcome when thou art judged".

CHAPTER 1

Deception

What is deception? Deception according to _Webster's Dictionary_ is a noun that means

1) the act of deceiving, 2) the fact or condition of being deceived, and 3) fraud or trick.What does it mean to deceive? According to _Webster's Dictionary,_ deceiving is a verb that means 1) to cause to believe an untruth, 2) to use or practice deceit and is synonymous with beguile, betray, delude, or mislead.

Deception in the Bible is first seen as the devil deceives Eve in the garden of Eden.

Genesis 3: 1-5 says, 1)"And he said unto the woman, Yea, hath God said, Ye shall not eat of every tree of the garden, 2) And the woman said unto the serpent,We may eat of the fruit of the trees of the garden, 3) But of the fruit of the tree which is in the midst of the garden,God hath said, Ye shall not eat of it, neither shall you touch it, lest ye die. 4) And the serpent said unto the woman, Ye shall not surely die: 5) For God doth know that in the day ye eat thereof, then your eyes shall be opened and ye shall be as gods, knowing good and evil".

After Eve ate of the fruit, and gave to her husband, Adam, and he did eat, this is what the Lord said unto the woman in Genesis 3:13, "And the Lord God said unto the woman, what is this that thou hast done? And the woman said, the serpent beguiled me, and I did eat". We now know that deception first started in the garden of Eden when the devil deceived Eve.

You will find the word deceived seventeen times in the Old Testament, and twelve times in the New Testament. Deception is throughout the Bible, especially the Old Testament.

According to the scriptures, all deception is not of the devil. Ezekiel 14:9 says, "And if the prophet be deceived when he hath spoken a thing, I the Lord have deceived that prophet, and I will stretch out my hand upon him, and will destroy him from the midst of my people Israel". This passage of scripture verifies that God himself deceives people according to His own will. II Thessalonians 2:11 states, "And for this cause God shall send them strong delusion, that they should believe a lie". According to *Webster's Dictionary,* the word delusion means deluding or being deluded, and the word delude means to mislead, deceive, or trick.

Let us now look at how the church body is being deceived concerning "The Rapture".

CHAPTER 2

Views

The teaching of views on "The Rapture" is the main reason the church is deceived. The Bible tells us in Proverbs 3:5, "Lean not to your own understanding", but we have not done that on this matter of "The Rapture". Here are some of the views people have concerning the Rapture: 1) Pre-tribulation

2) Post-tribulation

3) Partial Rapture

4) Mid-tribulation

Views have no place in God's house. Here is what Paul's letter to Timothy said about things of that sort. II Timothy 4:3-4 states, 3) "For the time will come when they will not endure sound doctrine, but after their own lusts shall they heap to themselves teachers, having itching ears; 4)And they shall turn away their ears from the truth, and shall be turned unto fables".

The word "fable" in *Webster's Dictionary* means falsehood. What we should do is believe what is written in the Bible. I have discovered that whatever you are looking for in the scriptures, you will find, even though it isn't there. (I hope you understand what I just said).

There are written scriptures in the Bible that tell us about Jesus' return. If we don't know these things, don't voice your views, but study so you can rightly divide the word of truth. Views expressed on a verse that is written is not the truth. Only that which is written is true. That's why it is stated in II Timothy 3:16,

"All scripture is given by inspiration of God, and is profitable for doctrine, for reproof, for correction, for instruction in righteousness".

I Corinthians 14:33 states, "For God is not the author of confusion, but of peace, as in all churches of the Saints". Present only the facts that are written in the word of God. Jesus corrected satan with only what is written in the word of God. St. Matthew 4: 4, 7, 10 states, "It is written".

Philippians 2:5 states, "Let this mind be in you, which was also in Christ Jesus". Jesus didn't use views. He used the written word of God. He is our example, so we are going to use the written word of God to show when "The Rapture" shall occur.

CHAPTER 3

The Coming of the Lord

The coming of the Lord to gather together his church is not hidden from us in the scriptures. What we have to know and always remember when studying scripture is that "Truth never disagrees with truth". For some of you brothers and sisters in the Lord that have never heard that before, I will say it again, "Truth never disagrees with truth". Truth always agrees with truth. Only that which is untrue, will disagree with truth. Always keep that in mind when studying the Bible.

In the sixth chapter of St. John's gospel, the word of truth tells us what day Jesus will raise his people up. In other words, it tells us what day Jesus will return. So let us take a look at St. John, sixth chapter. Jesus had just fed the five thousand and is now teaching in the synagogue at Capernaum. Those same people he had fed came there looking for him and found him there teaching. Here is what Jesus says to them in verses 36 and 37 of St. John, chapter 6:

36) "But I said unto you, that ye also have seen me, and believe not.

37) "All that the Father giveth me shall come to me; and him that cometh to me I will in no wise cast out". So, Jesus tells them even though they have seen the miracles, they still don't believe on him. But, everyone that his Father gives him will come to him and he will not turn away.

Then Jesus states in St. John 6:39, "And this is the Father's will which hath sent me, that of all which he hath given me I should lose nothing, but should raise it up again at the last day. Jesus states in St. John 6: 40, "And this is the will of him that sent me, that everyone which seeth the Son, and believeth on him, may have everlasting life: and I will raise him up at the last day. In St. John 6: 44, Jesus states, "No man can come to me, except the Father which hath sent me draw him: and I will raise him up at the last day. In St. John 6: 54, Jesus states, "Whoso eateth my flesh, and drinketh my blood, hath eternal life; and I will raise him up at the last day. We now know that Jesus will return and gather together his church body at the last day. We know it will not be in parts but all that his Father hath given him. The word of truth has said this four times in St. John's gospel, chapter 6 verses 39, 40, 44, and 54.

Jesus told this to all of his followers and we know this by what Martha said to him in St. John 11:24. Martha's brother Lazarus had died and she said to Jesus…24) I know that he shall rise again in the resurrection at the last day.

Remember that the word of truth will not disagree with the word of truth, but agree. So, wherever scripture is written concerning the day the Lord will be coming for his church body, it will be in agreement with the last day. Just as St. John 11:24 agrees with St. John 6:39, 40, 44, and 54, all scriptures in the Old Testament and New Testament concerning this matter will do the same. God is not the author of confusion, but of peace, as in all churches of the saints (I Corinthians 14:33).

When will the last day occur? To answer that question, we must first understand that at the last day is referring to only one day. There is the last day of the week, the last day of the month, and the last day of the year. They are all one day. The last day is also only one day instead of many days.

To find out when that last day will occur, let us begin at the 24th chapter of St. Matthew starting with the 3rd verse. St. Matthew 24:3

states, "And as he sat upon the Mount of Olives, the disciples came unto him privately, saying, tell us when shall these things be? And what shall be the sign of thy coming, and of the end of the world?"

The disciples ask Jesus about three things, but we are only concerned about one of these, what shall be the sign of thy coming? In answering their questions, Jesus will let them know when that last day will occur. Here is what Jesus says to them in St. Matthew 24th chapter, verses 27-31, 40 and 41; 27) For as the lightning cometh out of the east, and shineth even unto the west; so shall also the coming of the Son of man be; 28) For wheresoever the carcase is, there will the eagles be gathered together; 29) Immediately after the tribulation of those days shall the sun be darkened, and the moon shall not give her light, and the stars shall fall from heaven, and the powers of the heavens shall be shaken; 30) And then shall appear the sign of the Son of man in heaven: and then shall

all the tribes of the earth mourn, and they shall see the Son of man coming in the clouds of heaven with power and great glory; 31) And he shall send his angels with a great sound of a trumpet, and they shall gather together his elect from the four winds, from one end of heaven to the other; 40) Then shall two be in the field; the one shall be taken, and the other left; 41) Two women shall be grinding at the mill; the one shall be taken, and the other left.

Verse 29 of chapter 24 of St. Matthew lets us know when the last day will occur; it is immediately after the tribulation of those days. In verse 30, you see the Son of man coming in the clouds of heaven with power and great glory. In verse 31, he sends his angels to gather together his elect, which is the resurrection of the dead and the rapturing out of the saints who are living in verses 40 and 41.

St. Matthew, chapter 24, verses 29-31, are in perfect agreement with St. John chapter 6, verses 39, 40, 44, and 54. These verses not only show that it occurs at the last day, but they also let you know when that last day shall occur. The occurrence is after the tribulation.

If other scripture was in disagreement with the last day in the 6th chapter of St. John's gospel, verses 39, 40, 44, and 54 and the 29th verse of the 24th chapter of St. Matthew, after the tribulation, it would make the word of truth untrue. Then, Jesus, who said these things, would not be who he is, making the Bible untrue. But, we know the Lord is who he says he is; the way, the truth, and the life (St. John 14:6). We, who believe in his word, know what is said in St. John 6:39, 40, 44, 54 and St. Matthew 24: 27-31, 40 and 41 is true. Therefore, the scriptures that speak about the coming of the Lord for his church will agree. The Bible is the word of truth and truth agrees with truth.

In the book of St. Mark, chapter 13, verses 3 and 4, it states, 3) And as he sat upon the Mount of Olives over against the temple, Peter and James and John and Andrew asked him privately. 4) Tell us when shall these things be? and what *shall* be the sign when all these things shall be fullfilled? St. Mark tells us that these questions were asked by Peter, James, John, and Andrew. When we look back at St. Matthew 24:3, it tells us the disciples came and asked these questions, but St. Mark named the disciples. St. Mark 13: 3-4 agrees with St. Matthew 24:3.

St. Mark 13:24-27 states, 24) But in those days, after that tribulation, the sun shall be darkened and the moon shall not give her light; 25) And the stars of heaven shall fall, and the powers that are in heaven shall be shaken; 26) And then shall they see the Son of man coming in the clouds with great power and glory; 27) And then shall he send his angels, and shall gather together his elect from the four winds, from the uttermost part of the earth to the uttermost part of heaven.

Matthew and Mark are two different men whom the Lord used in writing their books about the gospel of Jesus Christ. Matthew was a tax collector who was sitting at the receipt of custom: and Jesus said unto him, "Follow me". And the Bible says, he arose, and followed him (St. Matthew 9:9). Matthew became one of the twelve disciples of Jesus Christ. Mark, who was called John Mark, was Barnabas' nephew. Barnabas is the person who took Paul and brought him to the apostles and declared unto them how he had seen the Lord in the way, when all of the disciples were afraid of him (Acts 9:26-27). Later on when Paul and Barnabas had a disagreement, they parted ways. Paul took Silas with him and Barnabas took his nephew, John Mark, with him.

It is believed that the book of St. Matthew was written around A.D. 37 and St. Mark was written around A.D. 57. But the verses about the coming of the Lord in both gospels are almost identical. St. Matthew and St. Mark are in agreement with the coming of the Lord at the last day, after the tribulation, to get his church body. Therefore, St. Mark 13: 24-27 is in agreement with St. John 6:39, 40, 44, and 54.

Before we look at the book of St. Luke, let us first take a careful look at Luke's early ministry. Luke was an associate of Paul doing his ministry. In Paul's second letter to Timothy, verse 11, chapter 4, he tells Timothy that only Luke is with him. That is the same Luke in Colossians chapter 4, verse 14, when Paul refers to Luke as the beloved physician.

Luke tells his account by saying in the 17th chapter of St. Luke, verse 24, "For as the lightning, that lighteneth out of the one part under heaven, shineth unto the other part under heaven; so shall also the Son of man be in his day". This is the exact same way that St. Matthew chapter 24, verse 27 begins. It has the same wording. Therefore, both are in agreement with one another. St. Luke 17:37 states, "Wheresoever the body is, thither will the eagles be gathered together." That verse is the same as St. Matthew 24:28 which states, "For wheresoever the carcase is, there will the eagles be gathered together. Luke didn't put in his writing the words "after the tribulation". The words that Luke stated in St. Luke 17:26 -30 were 26) And as it was in the days of Noe, so shall it be also in the days of the Son of man; 27) They did eat, they drank,they married wives, they were given in marriage, until the day that Noe entered into the ark, and the flood came, and destroyed them all; 28) Likewise also as it was in the days of Lot; they did eat, they drank, they bought, they sold, they planted, they builded; 29) But the same day that Lot went out of Sodom it rained fire and brimstone from heaven, and destroyed them all; 30) Even thus shall it be in the day when the Son of man is revealed. The same day that Jesus takes his church body out of the world, he fights the battle of Armageddon (Revelation 19: 17-21).

St. Luke tells us in verses 34-36 of chapter 17 about the rapturing of those saints who are living when Jesus comes for his church; 34) I tell you, in that night there shall be two men in one bed; the one shall be taken, and the other shall be left; 35) Two women shall be grinding together; the one shall be taken and the other left; 36) Two men shall be in the field; the one shall be taken, and the other left. St. Luke, chapter 17, verses 24, 26-29, 34-37 are in agreement about the last day with St. Matthew 24: 27-31, 40-41, St. Mark 13: 24-27, and St. John 6:39, 40, 44, and 54. All of these verses refer to the same topic, the last day.

I Corinthians 15: 51-52 states; 51) Behold, I shew you a mystery; We shall not all sleep, but we shall all be changed; 52) In a moment, in the twinkling of an eye, at the last trump: for the trumpet shall sound, and the dead shall be raised incorruptible, and we shall be changed. Verse 52 is the same as verse 31 in chapter 24 of St. Matthew which states, "And he shall send his angels with a great sound of a trumpet, and they shall gather together his elect from the four winds, from one end of heaven to the other". This event occurs after the tribulation (St. Matthew 24:29) at the last day (St. John 6:39, 40, 44, and 54). By it ocurring on the last day of man's rule makes it the last trump. I Corinthians 15:51, "We shall not all sleep" and St. Matthew 24: 40-41, "Two in the field, one taken, two women in the mill, one taken" are the same.

The Lord would not tell his disciples one thing and tell Paul another concerning the time of his return. There is no untruth in Jesus, nor is there any confusion. You cannot take the word of truth in I Corinthians and make the word of truth in St. Matthew, St. Mark, St. Luke, and St. John untrue. That is simply impossible to do. You cannot receive understanding of the word of God until you believe the word of God. The word of God is that what is written. It is written in St. Matthew 24: 29 and St. Mark 13:24 that

Jesus will return after the tribulation for his elect, which is his church. It is not written in scripture where Jesus will return to gather together his church body at any other time. Believe God's word.

I Thessalonians 4:13-17 states; 13) But I would not have you to be ignorant, brethren, concerning them which are asleep, that ye sorrow not, even as others which have no hope; 14) For if we believe that Jesus died and rose again, even so them also which sleep in Jesus will God bring with him; 15) For this we say unto you by the word of the Lord, that we which are alive and remain unto the coming of the Lord shall not prevent them which are asleep; 16) For the Lord himself shall descend from heaven with a shout, with the voice of the archangel, and with the trump of God: and the dead in Christ shall rise first; 17) Then we which are alive and remain shall be caught up together with them in the clouds, to meet the Lord in the air: and so shall we ever be with the Lord.

I Thessalonians 4: 13-17 is the same as I Corinthians 15: 51-52, St. Matthew 24: 27-31, 40, 41, and St. John 6:39, 40, 44 and 54. In Paul's letters of I Corinthians and I and II Thessalonians, his writing of the coming of the Lord is worded differently but, there is no difference in his message than in the four gospels. I Thessalonians 3:13 states at the end of the verse, "at the coming of our Lord Jesus Christ with all his saints". I Thessalonians 4:14 states, "even so them also which sleep in Jesus will God bring with him". Both of these passages of scripture are the same. These are the spirits of the saints that have died in Christ. Jesus brings them back so they can go back into their bodies which are in the grave to be resurrected in the resurrection of the just at the last day. This lets us know that there will be no rapture until the last day, which is after the tribulation. The statement, all his saints, (I Thessalonians 3:13) refers to those who have died in Christ.

II Thessalonians 2: 1-8 states 1) Now we beseech you brethren, by the coming of our Lord Jesus Christ, and by our gathering together unto him; 2) That ye be not soon shaken in mind, or be troubled, neither by spirit, nor by word, nor by letter as from us, as that the day of Christ is at hand; 3) Let no man deceive you by any means: for that day shall not come, except there come a falling away first, and that man of sin be revealed, the son of perdition; 4) Who opposeth and exalteth himself above all that is called God, or that is worshipped; so that he as God sitteth in the temple of God, shewing himself that he is God; 5) Remember ye not, that, when I was yet with you, I told you these things?; 6) And now ye know what withholdeth that he might be revealed in his time; 7) For the mystery of iniquity doth already work: only he who now letteth will let, until he be taken out of the way; 8) And then shall that wicked be revealed, whom the lord shall consume with the spirit of his mouth, and shall destroy with the brightness of his coming.

I will now explain each verse of II Thessalonians 2:1-8 to display a clear understanding of what is being said. 1) Paul is telling the "church of the Thessalonians", (II Thessalonians 1:1) about the Lord coming to gather together his church body. 2) Paul is saying to them, if someone was to say by word of mouth or by letter that Jesus could come anytime, it is just not true, do not believe them, and do not let it worry you. 3) Paul tells them in verse 3, that those people in verse 2 that say and write such things, are deceiving people, and for them not to be deceived by them, or any other means. He tells them two things must happen before that day comes. The second one is that the man of sin will be revealed. Until that man of sin be revealed, that day will not come. So the church will know without a doubt who that man is before the coming of the Lord. 4) Paul is telling how this man will speak against God and exalt himself above God. When the Jews build the temple of God, during trouble times in the tribulation, he will sit in the temple of God, and declare himself to be God. 5) Paul reminds them to keep in their rememberance the things he had told them concerning the coming of the Lord. 6) Paul tells them that they now know what is holding it back. 7) Paul tells them that wickedness was already at work. He who letteth work, will continue to let it work, until he be taken out of the way. 8) After he is taken out of the way, then that wicked shall be revealed. Paul tells them that the Lord will destroy that wicked one with the brightness of his coming.

There are those who say the church has to be raptured out of the world in order for the Holy Spirit to be removed, and they are using verse 7 for that reasoning. Verse 7 tells us that he will be taken out of the way, and not out of the world. It tells us in verse 3 that the man of sin has to be revealed and known by the church before Jesus comes. What they say contradicts what is said in verse 3. Revelation 13:7 also lets us know that this is not true. Revelation 13:7 says, "And it was given unto him to make war with the saints, and to overcome them."

These are the saints in Revelation 20:4 that were beheaded for the witness of Jesus, and for the word of God. Daniel 7:21-22 says, 21) "I beheld, and the same horn made war with the saints, and prevailed against them; 22) until the Ancient of days came, and judgement was given to the saints of the most High; and the time came that the saints possessed the kingdom".

With the man of sin prevailing against the saints and the saints being beheaded by him, this ended the time of the Gentiles and the Israelites (Jews) as a nation was graffed back into the vine. The work of the Holy Spirit is not finished, because he still has Jews to save. Jesus says this to the Jews in St. Matthew 23: 39, "For I say unto you, ye shall not see me henceforth, till ye shall say, Blessed is he that cometh in the name of the Lord".

Paul tells the church of the Thessalonians in verse 8 of II Thessalonians, chapter 2, that the Lord shall destroy that man of sin with the brightness of his coming. Once the man of sin is destroyed, the tribulation period is over. The tribulation period ends with his destruction. After the tribulation ends, the resurrection of the just will follow. Then the rapturing of those saints who are living at that time will occur. Following that, the Lord will fight the battle of Armageddon. II Thessalonians 2:8 is the same as St. Matthew 24: 27-30, and it agrees with St. John 6: 39, 40, 44, and 54

CHAPTER 4

Who is the Church?

The church is a body of baptized believers (Mark 16:16), born again, of water and of the Spirit (St. John 3:5), who believe on Jesus Christ the Son of God (St. John 3:16) whose sins have been forgiven (Colossians 2:13), those who have been predestined and called according to his purpose (Romans 8:28-29). They are a new creature (Galatians 6:15), a peculiar people who have been redeemed by the Lord (Titus 2:14). The church is those who are rooted and grounded in Jesus Christ (Ephesians 3:17). They are those who have had a renewing of the mind (Ephesians 4:23), and are no longer who they used to be (Ephesians 4:24), keeping their minds stayed on Jesus as they press toward the mark for the prize of the high calling of God in Christ Jesus (Philippians 3:14), the author and finisher of their faith (Hebrews 12:2). They are a city on a hill, a light in a dark world (St. Matthew 5:14), a loving family because God is love (1 John 4:8) and have taught his children to love (I Thessalonians 4:9). They are in the world, but not of the world (St. John 17:16), looking for that blessed hope, and the glorious appearing of the great God and their savior Jesus Christ (Titus 2:13). No longer friends of the world (James 4:4), they have become more than conquerors through him that loved them (Romans 8:37). They no longer lean to their own understanding (Proverbs 3:5), nor do they walk in the counsel of the ungodly, nor standeth in the way of sinners, nor sitteth in the seat of the scornful, but their delight is in the law of the Lord (Psalm 1:1-2). The church is an obedient people (Hebrews 5:9), a righteous people (Romans 5:19), those who love the Lord Jesus Christ (Ephesians 6:24) and love his commandments (II John 1:6). They are justified by faith (Romans 5:1) making them the children of God (Galatians 3:26). The church is the just who live by faith (Galatians 3:26).

The just are those who are of the faith. The just started with Abel in the Old Testament. Hebrews 11:4 says, "By faith Abel offered unto God a more excellent sacrifice than Cain, by which he obtained witness that he was righteous, God testifying of his gifts: and by it he being dead yet speaketh". Hebrews 11:13 lets us know that the saints in the Old testament died in faith, not having received the promises, but having seen them afar off and were persuaded of them, and embraced them, and confessed that they were strangers and pilgrims on the earth. The just ends with those saints that Jesus raptures out at the last day (St. Matthew 24: 40-41). Hebrews 11:

40 says, "God having provided some better thing for us, that they (Old Testament saints) without us should not be made perfect. Now we know that the saints in the Old Testament will not be made perfect without the saints in the New Testament. We will all be made perfect together because we are one body in Christ Jesus, and that body is the church. Therefore, the church begins with Abel and ends with the rapturing of the saints at the last day.

CHAPTER 5

The Rapture

Immediately after the tribulation, there will be the resurrection of the just and the rapturing of the saints who are living. They will be caught up together in the clouds, to meet the Lord in the air. They will be forever with the Lord. Those saints who will be in the rapture are Jews. The time of the Gentiles has passed. St. Matthew 24: 40-41 and St. Luke 17: 34-36 tells us of the Rapture, which will be on the last day of man's rule. Amen

Printed in the United States
By Bookmasters